For Mildred H[...] [...]rm
regard and the [...] [...] [...]
will derive some smiles from
these pages.

Irene Warsaw.

WARILY WE ROLL ALONG

Also by the Author:

A Word in Edgewise

IRENE WARSAW

Warily We Roll Along

THE GOLDEN QUILL PRESS
Publishers

Francestown   New Hampshire

Library of Congress Catalog Card Number 79-89587

ISBN 0-8233-0301-2

Printed in the United States of America

CONTENTS

ACKNOWLEDGMENTS

Grateful acknowledgment is made to the following, in which some of the poems included in this book were first published: *The American Legion Magazine,* Arizona Poetry Society, Burroughs Clearing House, *Chatelaine, The Christian Home, The Christian Science Monitor, Denver Post Empire Magazine, Good Housekeeping, IEA News, Journal of the American Medical Assn., The Lyric, Maclean's, McCall's, Modern Maturity,* National Federation of State Poetry Societies, *Nation's Business, The Ohio Motorist,* Pennsylvania Poetry Society, *Philadelphia Sunday Bulletin,* Poetry Society of Michigan, Poetry Society of New Hampshire, *Poetry View — Post Crescent, The Rotarian, The Saturday Evening Post* and *The Wall Street Journal.*

WARILY WE ROLL ALONG

LEND ME YOUR EAR (WITH PRIME INTEREST)

One picture, an old Chinese proverb maintains,
   Is better than ten thousand words,
But I'm not in line for pictorial gains
   And view this as all for the birds.
Photography skills I am strictly without;
   To laughter my art would impel you;
So what I have done or am thinking about
   In ten thousand words I will tell you.

PERPETUAL COMMOTION

Where are the wrongs we
    attacked with such vigor?

Where are the problems that
    once were so vital?

RIGHT HERE — we are fighting them
    yet, but they're bigger

And each has a fancier,
    updated title.

WRITE ON

It's quite a literary feat
To make a treatise seem a treat.

LET ME KNOW WHAT I THINK

A government mogul preparing a speech
Need never be stumped for decisions he'll reach.
He's told what he'll say and how well he will score
By news commentators a few days before.

OFF AND ON

I like the lines that speak of those
Who have no ethics or religions,
For whom some kind Burbankian guy
Should crossbreed books with homing pigeons.
If this occurs, and borrowed books
Start winging homeward by themselves,
The traffic, I confess, will be
As lively FROM as TO my shelves.

TOME, SWEET TOME

I'm grateful for your interest, friend,
    And now I am returning
The book you felt would benefit
    My scanty store of learning.
Your worry for its safe return
    Was plain from things you said,
But see — it's quite untorn, unmarked,
    Unsullied . . . . and unread.

SUNKEN GARDENERS

Our maiden attempt at a garden, last year,
   Was fervid but unscientific.
Some plantings maliciously failed to appear
   While others were grossly prolific.

Our string beans and lettuce and radishes grew
   With vigor and speed quite incredible,
But anything somewhat exotic or new
   Displayed not a sprig that was edible.

Our garden is gone. We have sodded the space
   And our zeal for the project is sodden.
The insects and weeds may take over the place
   Unfettered, unsprayed and untrodden.

This year there's no lopsided harvest to reap.
   We're humbled but not inconsolable.
The produce we buy is a long way from cheap
   But the intake is sweetly controllable.

ONE HIT, ONE ERROR

Rainy day — the thunder roars;
Kiddies cannot play outdoors.
Tired of books and quiet toys,
Want some exercise and noise.
Try an indoor baseball game;
Wind-up . . pitch . . defective aim.
Fearful crash — the glass goes popping.
Mom and Dad go window shopping.

THE MAIL OF THE SPECIES

When we dispatch
Our small donations
Results are prompt:
Solicitations
From other hungry
Corporations.

MERRILY I'LL ROLL, IF I
DON'T ROCK

I saw an ad for pills today
And sped my order on its way.
No ache or wheeze I've ever had
Has been neglected in the ad.
So many age-effects and ills
Strike those who fail to take the pills
That I can't help but wonder how
I've kept in motion up to now.
If I can manage to survive
Until the magic pills arrive,
Farewell, old peer group on the skids.
I'll be cavorting with the kids.

LIES OF LEAST RESISTANCE

I'd like our twenty-year-old game
    Still more if it were true
When I insist you look the same
    And you swear I do too.

WEATHER BEATEN

We put a little cash away
To guard against a rainy day.
It didn't help an awful lot —
A rainy *year* was what we got.

BUY-PASSED

These days, it is rather astounding to me
To check the securities market and see
The prices of stocks on my own special list
And bountiful dividend rates that exist.
My pets have proved even more lush than I thought
    them —
I find I'd be wealthy today, had I bought them.

BULLISH, BEARISH OR SHEEPISH

We don't need to study the stock market page
To know when the blue chips go soaring or fall.
We glance at our handy, reliable gauge —
The look on the face of the boss tells it all.

I'LL TAKE IT LYING DOWN

The state of sleep is still mysterious
Though scientists have long been serious
In efforts to assess the role
That conscious thought does not control,
When sleep possesses us at night
And puts us *out* as any light.
They know a healthy outlook stems
From periodic dream-world REM's,
But some activities occur
Whose psychic force remains a blur.

If ever doctors should require
My services, I'm up for hire.
I'll happily arrange to sleep
Beside their charts and try to keep
My REM's at work and on the ball,
Reporting items I recall.
This seems, as occupations go,
A dreamy way to earn some dough.

PROCEED AT YOUR OWN RISK

I'm leery of stints I've not tackled before
And so getting old is a fate I deplore.
What's more, the alternative holds no appeal —
That too is an untried (and breathtaking) deal.

REAL GONE

My own brand of name-dropping
   Never gets brash —
Names drop from my memory
   Quick as a flash.

HORSE SENSE

I've read of the benefit fiber food brings
And firmly believe what the doctors are saying.
I'm eating such wheaty and oatmealy things
That one of these days, I expect, I'll be neighing.

CARNIVORE ON THE MUSCLE

There's nothing wrong with good, familiar hash or Irish
    stew.
What gets him is the souped-up and exotic sort of brew
Concocted from a recipe of multiple-ingredient
Complexness that the sturdy carnivore deems inexpedient
He doesn't care for wines and herbs and relishes and
    sauces
Combined to make a hodgepodge into which the gourmet
    tosses,
With wild presumption, honest meat to marinate or
    simmer.
The carnivore, becoming ever hungrier and grimmer,
Deplores (albeit fruitlessly) the culinary tussle
That smothers the identity of organ and of muscle.
He dreams of dinner parties with a staunch, old-fashioned
    host
Who serves what can be recognized as steak or chop or
    roast —
Not mangled, not awash with goo, not camouflaged with
    spices,
But lovely on his plate in self-respecting chunks or slices.
He wants uncomplicated meat that looks and tastes like
    meat.
Neat.

UNREASONABLE FACSIMILE

Photographers no more display
The care and art they used to show.
I never get results today
Like those of twenty years ago.

MAIL ORDER — AND CHAOS

The catalog through which we buy
A gadget seems to notify
Its fourteen cousins of the sale,
And — pronto — all are in our mail.

THE MORE, THE WARIER

The more I'm advised, and the more things I read,
    And the more paths I follow the lure of,
The less I'm convinced of the way to proceed
    And the fewer opinions I'm sure of.

LOVE STORY

You're like an open book to me.
I mean, of course, a mystery
Contrived with such involved designs
It's hard to read between the lines.
In every kind of situation
I read with love and fascination.
Whenever I can spot a clue
That points to what you'll say or do
I'm apt to organize a smile
That's visible for half a mile,
But even when you make me frown
I simply CANNOT put you down.

WORDS AND THE WISE

The eager dictionary users
Who want their stock of words increased
Are nearly always those perusers
Who need the extra knowledge least.

COLD CALCULATION

Alarm bells always start to ring
Somewhere inside me when I'm told
Of scientists continuing
Their fight to whip the common cold.
I do not like to look ahead.
Some dismal day they'll be succeeding
And there will go my rest in bed,
My meals on trays, my peaceful reading.

ALL FOR ONE

Though talking to myself may seem
A little odd, I'm on the beam
And know which side of pro and con
My oratory's buttered on.
Opinion, bias, whimsy, fact —
My words stand firm and unattacked.
While other speakers get berated,
My audience is fascinated.

THE LITTLE THINGS WHO COUNT

The ones who look as though they need
To pay their calories no heed
Just possibly may look that way
From faithful heeding every day.

ONE COOK WHO CAN SPOIL THE
BROTH SINGLEHANDED

The reason I do not get fat
Is simple, clear, untwistable.
The undisputed fact is that
My cooking is resistible.

LOSERS WEEPERS? BAH!

It's true you now are lithe and thin,
But spare us that triumphant grin
And skip the glad descriptive prattle.
We *know* you won the losing battle.

ADVICE, BOILED DOWN BUT STILL TOUGH

Tips from the experts, if taken to heart,
Make eating a mixed-up and difficult art.
First, for inducing a keen appetite
Cocktails are nice or some soup is all right.
Use only foods of superior grade
And learn how delectable flavors are made.
Marinate, garnish, sauté, dredge and dip;
Toast, bake or simmer; stir gently or whip.
Copy the world's irresistible dishes,
Omitting no trimmings that make them delicious.
Serve things attractively. Note eye appeal —
Color-plan foods for a more tempting meal.
Having observed and accomplished all that,
Try not to eat much or you will get fat.

LOVE LAUGHS AT LOCKOUTS

Household Hint: Wrap an extra house key in aluminum foil and "plant" it in the ground near the house where it will be easy to find the next time someone in the family is locked out. The key will remain clean and dry in the foil. A drop of oil on it also will discourage rust. (From a Family Magazine)

You mean we're locked out? Our keys are inside?
Well, dear, I have news and I tell it with pride.
I planted a key in the ground somewhere near!
Now, just let me think — it was right around here.
What's wrong, dear? You're suddenly not on your mettle.
I thought at the party you seemed in high fettle.
I cannot see why you should sound so disgusted.
The key, when we find it, won't even be rusted.
I wisely anointed the thing with fresh oil
And wrapped it in shiny aluminum foil
And planted it. Darling, now please don't get sore.
I went slightly north — or else south — from the door.
It's rather too bad that there's not a full moon;
It's frightfully dark. Oh, I've dug up a spoon!
You used to adore being up all night long;
You shouldn't complain — you're so vital and strong.
Go on — give that shovel a healthier push.
Look out! You're uprooting the spirea bush!
Just look at that glow on the eastern horizon.
Now THAT is a sight you can sure feast your eyes on.
This beautiful weather is long overdue.
I love being up for the sunrise, don't you?
Now don't use that tone and don't start a tirade.

No doubt you think I am *in love* with this spade.
At least we can see since the coming of dawn,
But *look* what you've done to our velvety lawn.
I don't like your language. I'm horribly shocked.
Why — look, dear! How lucky! The door wasn't locked.

HEAR TODAY, GONE TOMORROW

To close one's mind to facts is wrong.
Whenever knowledge comes along
    I'm eager to annex it;
But knowledge doesn't seem to find
Repose within my open mind.
    It seeks the nearest exit.

SHORE LINES

Oh, don't give a thought to the water and sand!
    Come into the house, though you're dripping,
For here at the beach we're a lighthearted band
    With our picnicking, sunning and dipping.

I firmly believe we should frolic and rest here,
Ignoring the clutter. (I too am a guest here.)

HEAD LINES

Man's dome-shaped skull is built to guard
His brain. This dome is very hard
Which helps it keep, though soundly whacked,
Its precious load (the brain) intact.
The workings of the brain would suffer
More often if it had no buffer;
It functions, as is manifest,
With strange meanderings at best.

TWO LEGS TO STAND ON

From Bering Strait to Libya
Each human needs a tibia
(In fact, he needs a pair of them).
This bone helps form a sort of stem
That fits the space, as you can see,
Between the ankle and the knee;
And if it were not there at all
Man probably would have to crawl.

WELL-PLANNED DURABILITY

Man's heart, no bigger than his fist,
If absent would be sorely missed.
Inside his chest a gentle thumping
Assures man that his heart is pumping.
Its constant, rhythmic beats propel
His blood to every body cell,
A process known as circulation.
This should occur without cessation.
Since man can't live without his heart,
He's lucky that this vital part
In every single case supplies
Its pumping action till he dies.

O, MY ACHING BACK

I'm awed by the treatments bright doctors devise
    And cures that result from their labors —
Miraculous knowledge that never applies
    To me or my kin, friends and neighbors.

THEY MAKE ME LIKE TIRED

Sometimes I'd like to clout
The youthful friend or kin
Whose talk is so far out
It makes me feel all in.

RAZZ-MA-TAZZ, AND ALL THAT JAZZ

I tackle each new crop of slang,
Ask meekly for the kids' translations,
And do my best to get the hang
Of all those zany conversations.
I get things firmly fixed in mind
Right on the dot, six months behind.

THE STRAIN OF MUSIC

With here-and-now music, it's good to think young
And no one's more willing than I.
I'm up on what's tootled and tinkled and sung —
What stumps me completely is WHY.

JOHNNY-GO-LATELY

Here lies John Doe, of doubtful fame.
Ten thousand no ones bore his name,
　　Ten thousand more will bear it.
When lack of good identity
Surrounds a man, the law says he
　　Shall take a name and wear it,
And so in varied form and face
John Doe pops up most any place —
　　In gutter, glen and garret.
Here lies Anonymous at rest,
A borrowed name his one bequest —
　　How GOOD of him to share it.

THE SHOW MUST GO ON — AND ON

No doubt comedians in long-run plays
Grow weary of repeating funny gags
And sometimes even feel pronounced malaise
From too-familiar tales that dog the wags.

MINE ARE TOO TRUE FOR WORDS

I know the humble role you play
Is good for laughs and most disarming.
The self-belittling things you say
Are cute, untrue and always charming.
I'm jealous, but I'm not about
To try that kind of OH-POOR-ME-ing.
The seeds of thought I'd plant might sprout —
I might find all my friends agreeing.

NO SOONER SAID THAN RUED

When clumsy or inept remarks
    Spring from me like a fountain,
Just watch me squirm and try to make
    A molehill of a mountain.

HUE TO THE LINES

He's constantly faced with the burden
   (No wonder he can't get ahead)
Of keeping himself in the pink
   And his finances out of the red.

SAVING ACCOUNT

I keep all my pencils, no matter how small.
I save lengths of string on a big, lumpy ball.
I fold wrapping paper and stow it in bales,
Collect rubber bands and all sizes of nails.
I store nuts and bolts, slightly beat, in their box
And hang on to keys which don't fit any locks.
Glass jars, empty spray cans — I'm happy to see 'em
All stashed in the nooks of my bulging museum.
I'm thrifty that way, and I stoutly refuse
To throw away something I might want to use;
But I CANNOT hang on to, save, stow, store or stash
Cash.

PARLIAMENTARY OUTLAW

When clubs have a weighty decision at stake
And factional argument checks it,
A motion I'm tempted to quietly make
Is one which will lead to the exit.

ON THE RUN

Two types in which
Club members come:
Some run for office,
Some run from.

THERE'S ALWAYS A SQUARE PEG
AT A ROUND TABLE

Plans are attempted for all situations
From neighborhood picnic to foreign relations
In meetings of various sizes and kinds
That lack, all too often, a meeting of minds.

UNEARTHLY SENTIMENTS

It may be absurd, but I don't like to fly.
The earth doesn't wobble as much as the sky.
I've looked down on clouds of rare beauty and form
But view LOOKING UP to see clouds as the norm.
My faith in the engines transcends silly doubt.
Still, if they should falter I'd like to peer out
At good, solid concrete my feet can explore
Six inches below, if I open a door.
A city looks strange when I'm high in the air
And muster the courage to see if it's there.
It's certainly true that I get somewhere fast
By flying, and once the brave venture is past
A wonderful smugness pervades flesh and bone.
I don't like to fly, but I love *having flown*.

DOUBLE TAKE

They say he has his mother's eyes,
    Her hair, her crooked grin.
He got his father's walk and size
    And fine, determined chin.

The lad, with teen-age growing pains
    He shares with everyone,
Is sure he got his parents' brains
    And left them both with none.

A LITTLE BACK TALK

A cord runs through the human spine
To keep its stack of bones in line.
The bones, in turn, do much to keep
Man vertical when not asleep.
As evolution's march progressed
This kind of backbone worked out best
And still today it faithfully
Makes vertebrates of you and me.

CHEMO MEMO

Man's liver is a brownish blob
That does a most prodigious job.
It manufactures gall, or bile,
And normally keeps some on file
Stored neatly in a pear-shaped sac.
From there the liver's yields attack
The food man eats, to change its state
By methods man can't duplicate
Or even halfway understand.
He ought to treat this outsize gland
With due respect and loving care
To keep it in topnotch repair,
Because to get along at all
Man needs an awful lot of gall.

MOPE, AND YOU MOPE ALONE
(At Least I Do)

When I'm not feeling brisk and gay
My friends should flock around and cheer me,
But things do not work out that way.
That's when they can't stand being near me.

THINGS TO DO TODAY

I do not ask advice of friends
  As often as I should —
I never listen, but it tends
  To make them feel so good.

STICK-TO-IT-IVE-NESS

When cooking, I produce some flops.
  I do the best I can
But still come up with naked chops
  And breaded frying pan.

WE TURN THEM OFF, AND VICE VERSA

With energy in short supply
We try to do our bit — we buy
Low-wattage bulbs and hope we'll be
No drag upon the G. N. P.
Such half-size bulbs in every room
Produce a sort of gentle gloom
Which makes it hard, we all admit,
To not keep *twice as many* lit.

WAITING GAME

A conscience is what makes it hard
For thrifty people to discard
Left-over food. These careful souls
Store little dabs in little bowls
And quite serenely pitch them later
When cleaning the refrigerator,
Achieving thus a double feat:
They feel first dutiful, then neat.

ACCIDENTS WILL HAPPEN — EVEN GOOD ONES

Okay. You fixed the washer, dear,
And my regard for you is high,
But don't be smug and cavalier —
You're just as much surprised as I.

I AM THE OTHERS' KEEPER

Dear canner of foods, what selecting you did!
You used an impractical, difficult lid.
Your jar is unhandy. Its mouth is so small
Refilling it wouldn't be easy at all —
In fact, I'd be plunged into one of my moods
By trying to use it for left-over foods.
That bulge at its base (a delight to the eye)
Is pesky to wash, even harder to dry.
Your lovely container brings joy to my day:
I'll briskly, unguiltily throw it away.

NEWS CONFERENCE

We met, shoving carts, in a food store today.
"Hi, neighbor," she cried in her nice, cheery way.
"What's new? Oh, I know you have worked mighty hard.
That's clear from one look at that fabulous yard!
Your house looks superb with that delicate green —
A lovelier paint job I never have seen.
Stop in for a visit. I simply can't stand
Not knowing the news and what else you have planned
To perk up your place!" Then her cart and her smile
Took off and were lost in that populous aisle.

Her praise sounded great, but there isn't a doubt
That one of these days the dear soul will find out
Some news of the sort she's so eager to know:
We moved from her neighborhood six months ago.

SOBER THOUGHT

At home, on the job, and in public affairs
I wrestle like fury with problems and cares.
They're jarring, in view of the trouble I go to —
They drive me to drink and leave no time or dough to.

GO TO THE AUNT, THOU SLUGGARD

A maiden aunt is thought to be
Equated with a money tree
Whose branches bend with lovely weight
As fiscal fruits accumulate.
Young relatives are quite inclined
To have this dreamy crop in mind
When wanting stereo, or clothes,
Or car — whatever they suppose
Will make a life-style somewhere near
The status of some lucky peer.
These handouts bear the guise of loans
But spinster aunts know in their bones
That often in the stilly night
Such little deals sink out of sight.
(Well, surely sweet old aunts forget
A loving blood relation's debt!)
If needy kids are ineluctable
They should at least be tax deductible.

PULL YOURSELVES TOGETHER

Sometimes I have a queasy hunch
We've reached that population crunch.
Our neighbors' Open House last night
Left not an open *inch* in sight.

SPRING FERVOR

Some signs of spring that rarely fail
To meet the eye say: RUMMAGE SALE.

POLITICAL HORN OF PLENTY

They're not called whistle-stop campaigns
When candidates do not ride trains,
And yet that name is not far wrong.
They toot their own horns loud and long.

THE GOLDEN (AND YELLOW) RULE

I hug the straight and narrow path
That's marked by white or yellow lines —
I want no other driver's wrath,
No violation points, no fines.
When I am driving, count on me
For willing, meek cooperation.
One-third of this is courtesy,
Two-thirds is plain self-preservation.

THERE'S NEWS ON THE HOME FRONT TOO

You write me you're having a marvelous time,
    Your trip's doing wonders for you.
Well, whaddya know! I've discovered that I'm
    Enjoying the interval too.

CHANGE OF PACE

I once was a lighthearted viewer
Of diets, but now I feel bluer.
   I guard inch and ounce
    But my footfalls won't bounce
As they did when my years totalled fewer.

LOW-PRESSURE AREA

As work-force member he's quite bold.
He braves the winter's bitter cold,
A broiling sun, or rain, or wind,
Remarkably self-disciplined.
He labors with determined grin
To keep that pay check coming in.
On week ends, though, he finds it hard
To cope with tasks in house and yard.
Year-round, there's little he can do —
The weather's always much too TOO.

I'LL BE SEEING YOU

My glasses, in the frames I chose
Because I thought they flattered me,
Do little for the way I look
But very much for how I see.

DEFACED

He slept too late,
   Set such a pace
His razor slipped
   And he lost face.

THE BEAT GENERATION

I'm caught between two vocal femmes
   Whose views grow ever stronger.
My daughter wants to hoist my hems,
   My mother wants them longer.

CONTENTS NOTED, VAGUELY

The labels for things we are eating or using
Have technical language that's very confusing.
We're often in doubt whether points which they raise
Are meant as a warning or indicate praise.
A product has something extracted or added;
It's thickened or thinned or extended or padded;
It's soluble, flaky, pre-cooked or exploded;
It's blended, homogenized, lightened or loaded;
It's scented, deodorized, synthesized, sealed,
Astringent, extruded, infused or congealed;
It's filtered or fortified, strained or enriched —
And we are bewildered, befuddled, bewitched.

THE EARLY BIRD CATCHES THE SQUIRMS

Who felt very virtuous, back in July,
When shopping for Christmas gifts early?
    'Twas I.
Who now has on hand from that summertime spree
Completely unsuitable presents?
    'Tis me.

BRING IN THE OLD, BRING
OUT THE NEW

When Christmas is past
  And exchanges commence
Department store workers
  Remain present-tense.

RING OUT, WILD BELLS

O lucky world! From pole to pole
   As each old year departs
Timed perfectly to leave no hole
   A new year always starts.

ADIEU, ADIEU

Don't dally, Winter — you may go!
   You did your work with zest.
You must be weary. Pack your things,
   And have a lovely rest;
For Spring has sent blithe messengers
   To say that she is waiting.
Perhaps you saw — you must have heard —
   Those children roller skating.

SUGGESTION BOXED

The men in my life, eager souls that they are,
All offer advice for the care of my car.
Opinions are lengthy and firm as can be —
And not any two of them ever agree.

AUTOMATIC SHIFT

He doesn't care if ashes drop
Upon the rug or table top;
He leaves his books and papers where
They fall in heaps around his chair;
He sprawls upon the couch to snooze
Unmindful of his dusty shoes;
When he prepares the simplest drink
There's chaos in the kitchen sink.
But, oh — what care and neatness he'll
Demand when he's behind the wheel,
What slaves to tidiness we are
When riding in his precious car!

52

TEMPUS FIDGETS

A recent observation carries
The knockout punch for one fond dream:
I note that my contemporaries
Are older than I hope I seem.

I DON'T DIG IT

Although I pursue
    All suggestions as bidden,
My inner potential
    Stays stubbornly hidden.

TWENTY-PLUS-THIRTY VISION

It's not very cheering
    To note that somehow
My peer group is peering
    Through bifocals now.

ENCOUNTER WITH MY PHYSICIAN

How strange to see you so relaxed and gay
In sandals, slacks and brightly-printed shirt!
You are the star, as party guests display
Their joy in you as sparkling extrovert.
I, who have turned to you in pain or fear
And known your role as savior and clinician,
Am speechless with surprise at finding here
A second pedestal in firm position.
I am perplexed. I have no wish to cope
With views I must abandon or revise
To reach beyond white jacket, stethoscope,
And grave concern reflected in your eyes.
    Let your wit flash. Our senses are delighted.
    I laugh — and wish I had not been invited.

POSTMASTER: HANDLE WITH CARE

Our mailperson lately is cause for concern.
She's pregnant, as any observer can learn
By merely a glance at her contour and size.
A short leave of absence would seem very wise.
When I see her coming, I'm nudged by the fear
A Special Delivery may happen right here.

IN THE BAG

The bursa hangs around a joint
    In sac-like conformation.
Its contents ooze to give this point
    Important lubrication,
And if the joint reports a lack
    Of bursa juice to slide in
Bursitis may have found the sac
    Quite cozy to reside in.

DOUBLE EXPOSURE

When I recall a past event —
    Some flood or show or crime —
I briefly loathe someone who says,
    "That was before my time."

When people older still than I
    Indulge in backward-glancing,
I hold my tongue — but guess what thought
    Seems suddenly entrancing!

CAPSULE PUNISHMENT

When I have a cold or a wheeze or an ache
I like to describe the concoctions I take;
I like to discuss my injections and pills
And clothe with stark drama my everyday ills.
Possessed of an ailment I wish to explore,
There's nothing that frustrates and vexes me more
Than this bit: I hopefully say, "How are you?"
To someone whose symptoms are fabulous too
Who makes me behave and shut up about mine
By weakly and nobly replying, "I'm fine."

AT IT, HAMMER AND TONGUE

The carpenter who had to make
Repairs correcting HIS mistake
Used words and hammer angrily.
Mad at himself? Nope. Mad at ME.

ABSORBING PROBLEM

My car is showing signs of wear
But chugs away in any weather,
Repaying me for loving care
By friendly jaunts we take together.
We've both withstood a lot of jolts,
But no one ever comes along
With pistons, cables, nuts and bolts
To fix ME up when something's wrong.
I'm not exactly wearing out —
Just zapped by bumps I'm always facing,
Which makes it clear beyond a doubt
My shock absorbers need replacing.

MAN OF LETTERS

Dear postman, blue-clad, with your burden so sweet,
At last I can see you a block up the street!
I wait at my window, expectant and tense,
Enjoying this daily delightful suspense.
How faithful you are, and how great is your worth,
How friendly your smile — you're the salt of the earth.
No other employment, I'm certain, assures
A welcome as eager and joyous as yours.
Your progress seems slow but you're finally here,
Kind bearer of letters and envoy of cheer!

*　　*　　*　　*

The villain, the scoundrel, the monster, the sneak —
That's twice he has passed without stopping this week.

THE GIRLS WHO LEAVE ME BEHIND THEM

I'm reading a highly encouraging book.
It gives me a clubby, behind-the-scenes look
At glamorous female celebrities' lives
As artists, career women, mothers and wives.
They too have their struggles with woebegone ids,
With too little money, with vigorous kids.
They market, clean house, or get hit by a virus
And bravely go on to amuse or inspire us.
They do or make something (from lectures to pies)
And fame sort of happens. The author implies
That even by me such renown is achievable.
How jolly! How hopeful! And HOW unbelievable.

YOO-HOO, YOU U. F. O.

Today I got a glad hello
From someone I suppose I know —
The type whose image as he passes
Is Dash

      plus Beard

           plus Huge Dark Glasses.

VACATION WITH PAY-OFF

This is the season of joyous vacation,
Of egos restored to acceptable station
By people refreshingly thrilled to have met us,
Who can't bear to leave us, who promptly forget us.

UNFAIR

His physical ailments are rarely severe,
But more often minor and brief in duration.
With uncanny malice, they always appear
On holidays, week ends, and during vacation.

NO BARKING HERE TO CORNER, PLEASE

Our neighbors' dogs (a good-sized batch)
Are friendly mutts who'd never bite us,
But there are times we wish they'd catch
Nice, painless, chronic laryngitis.

AUTO INTOXICATION

He's being very sweet again;
    That gleam is in his eye.
He's feeling obsolete again
    And in a mood to buy.

New model cars are on display
    And he is all a-twitter.
The car we have is quite o. k.
    But short a little glitter.

His conscience will be shrinking now;
    His judgment's under par.
No logic mars his thinking now —
    He wants a brand-new car.

Revise the budget! Go in debt!
    Economize at home!
Do anything, just so we get
    That extra bit of chrome.

EASY DOES IT

The salesman gave me and my check a long look
   And then disappeared for a while.
I grumbled because of the time all this took;
   He worked up a halfhearted smile.
"The manager says we must do it that way.
   We have to be careful," said he.
How silly. To know if my check was o. k.
   Why didn't he simply ask ME?

AU JUS BRING ME SOME ROAST BEEF

One of the times you annoy me is when you
Expect me to read foreign words on the menu.

PARDON US IF WE SOUND DOGMATIC

We're patient, Fido, when you bark
Or leave your paw-prints on the floor.
A hundred times, from dawn to dark,
We let you in or out the door.
We're calm about the fur that flies
In little tufts around our feet,
But SCRAM with those pathetic eyes
Begrudging every bite we eat.

OUTREACH AND OVERREACH

Before his retirement he made a small vow
To stay in the swim and to think here-and-now.
He listed some causes he might volunteer
To work for, so people would know he's still here.
He hoped to help peck at injustice and cares
And stay in the mainstream of human affairs.

The *mainstream*? With jobs he was cunningly handed
Right smack in the *rapids* is where he has landed.

I CAME LIKE LION

Myself when young did eagerly frequent
The stores for every Clearance Sale event
    And, bearing merchandise in battered arms,
Came out with funds and self completely spent.

Anon, the Seed of Wisdom did I sow.
Self-preservation laboured it to grow
    Until this withered harvest I did reap:
"At bargain spots I quail; I will not go."

And when Thyself with aching foot shall drag
Among the zealots of the marked-down tag
    And in Thy fearful errand reach the spot
Where I made one, explode an empty bag.

TO THEE I CLING, JUST THE SAME

The tides in money matters show
A hectic ebb and not much flow.
On every hand I hear and see
The news of some big spending spree
And read with horrified distaste
Of bureaucratic graft and waste.
It makes me hot beneath my collar
To see how taxes gouge the dollar
For which John Doe and I have toiled —
The gravy train is kept well oiled.
My country's state may seem dismaying
But bid me no farewells. I'm staying.

ENDEAVOR

In spite of life's perplexities,
    From which I'm not exempt,
I swear I'll reach a ripe old age
    Or die in the attempt.

OVERHEAD AND UNDERHANDED

A crisis that pitches me into a tizzy
When I want to read or am otherwise busy
Is that which demands sudden action in dealing
A swift knockout blow to a bug on the ceiling.
What's neatest — to sweep, squirt or climb up and swat
Will contents of can or of bug leave a spot?
I scramble for weapons, return for the fight,
And find that the creature has slunk out of sight.
My fear doesn't vanish, as one might suppose —
In fact, with this shifty maneuver it grows.
Instead of the creep I was able to see
I feel two or three may have landed on me.

WISTFUL THINKING

Sometimes when life gets rather dull
Or even downright overcast
I tell myself at least this lull
Won't make a wish-I-hadn't past.

GROUP THERAPY

When some small illness picks on me
And won't respond to medication,
There's one unfailing remedy:
A sudden party invitation.

RECIPROCAL TRADE

Dear hosts, we'll remember this dinner forever
If you'll not appear too ambitious and clever.
Just serve us a filling and passable meal
From cans, or an instant or quick-frozen deal.
Don't drag out your elegant silver and dishes
For us — we have modest, unfinicky wishes
That don't call for formal, superior stuff.
Your cozy chitchat and some laughs are enough.
It's not very flattering treatment, that's true,
But what an excuse when we entertain you!

FIRST AIDE

We too can laugh at winter's storm
And sing of love that keeps us warm.
But, gosh — it's nice in spite of that
To have a trusty thermostat.

NAKED TRUTH

At beach resorts when days turn snappy
Vacationers become unhappy,
For all of them have come equipped
To spend the season weather-stripped.

THERE'S ALWAYS A HAND OUT
FOR A HANDOUT

We sometimes feel neglected
Or maybe even shunned
But never when some outfit
Decides to raise a fund.

TIME AND TIDINGS

I bought a book to help me read
At several times my present speed
And also help me comprehend
The meanings printed words intend.
The trouble is that I can't find
The time and discipline of mind
To read and grasp what I should know —
I'm too preoccupied and slow.
I need some way to help me read
The book at several times the speed
I now use and to comprehend
The meanings that its words intend.
The trouble is . . . .

THE MAN WITH THE HOE, MOWER,
RAKE OR SHOVEL

The nicest season of the year
Is any one of three NOT HERE.

TIME TAMED

When young, I sneered at good advice
And conscience paid a sticky price.
I was too foolish, vain and weak
To hear the voice of caution speak.
Now that I'm wise enough to heed it
Things sure have changed — I rarely need it.

SHOP TALK

Fortune cookies used to be
A merry little novelty,
But now we swallow fortune cake,
Fortune lettuce, fortune steak,
Fortune coffee, fortune pop.
A fortune's what it takes to shop.
And as for travel, clothes or car —
Unfortunate, that's what we are.

THE POET LECTURES AT A SEMINAR

He dazzles us. Concepts of form and rhyme
Are pierced with arrow-word and mocked with grin.
He flays the sonnet as a tool for crime
Or fourteen lines of base iambic sin.
The rondeau, villanelle and triolet
Are nice conceits for craftsmanship or play
But life's complexities cannot be met
With pretty lines that give no scope or sway.
He strides and blusters with such confidence,
Such verbal charm, persuasiveness and force,
Conservatives keep secret their defense
And tyros, blushing, view a sterner course.
    We read his work; his poems rhyme and scan.
    We love the brilliant, inconsistent man.

THE OUTCOME WAS INCOME

It's clear we were slipping a gasket
    In thinking he'd be a poor catch.
He put all his eggs in one basket
    And — darned if they didn't all hatch.

EVEN COMMON CENTS

Collecting coins is said to be
A popular activity.
At any rate, straight down the line
They're busily collecting mine.

SOMETHING VENTURED, NOTHING GAINED

We choose a stock, invest a bit,
And there the hopeful venture ceases.
While other people's holdings split,
Ours shatter into little pieces.

MANY A SLIP SLIPS

It's pleasant to stand in a little less awe
Of the world-renowned actress I recently saw.
We've something in common (not much, it is true):
She fought with an uncontrolled shoulder strap too.

MY MIRROR GIVES CAUSE FOR REFLECTION

Hope leaped inside me as I heard
Each confident, exciting word.
At last, went the announcer's line,
New youthful beauty could be mine.
Results would utterly amaze
My friends in only twenty days.
This was for ME, this glowing ad.
I grabbed a pen and memo pad
To pin down, when the moment came,
This wonder-working product's name.
And what good news fell on my ears?
I've used the silly stuff for years.

HER SUPPLY EXCEEDS MY DEMAND

She offers me a bit of news
   (She gathers more than I)
Or one of her familiar views
   And adds, "Don't ask me why!"
That brisk request is one she can
   Quite safely put an end to.
To ask her why is not my plan —
   I never do intend to.

FOUND AND LOST DEPARTMENT

If through a stroke of luck you find
The perfect product of its kind
(Detergent, face cream, car wax, food),
Maintain a deadpan face and mood.
No smiles, no cheers, no happy chatter —
Just make believe it doesn't matter,
Because should you so much as *grin* you'd
Find the item discontinued.

DISTANT EARLY WARNING

I smile upon bees as they pollinate trees
Some distance removed from my private abode.
My friendship is great for an ant and his mate
That stay in their hill by the side of the road.
The crawler that burrows or makes little furrows
To help our old earth absorb water and air
May work at his mission without opposition
If he will stick close to his diggings out there.
But a fly, beetle, spider or other outsider
That enters my dwelling to seek board and room
Is viewed as a squatter and whammed with a swatter
Or squirt-can or shoe into premature doom.

THE HANDWRITING ON THE WALLET

It helps to be rich,
The advantage of which
Lets a maiden or man
Woo catch as cash can.

FIRST ON THE AGENDA

A conclave or convention looms.
Men busily engage the rooms,
Appoint committees, plan citations;
Order meals, count reservations;
Arrange for speakers, workshops, forums;
Choose candidates; solicit quorums.
These tasks their wives will gladly share
Once they've decided what to wear.

I'LL TAKE NOW, THANK YOU

What's past is past, I always say,
So I refuse to reminisce
And moon about some bygone day
Insisting it was perfect bliss.
It isn't hard to steer my mind
Away from trips to way-back-when.
My life-style wasn't quite the kind
For which I have a dreamy yen.

DRIVING DESIRE

I hold my breath and aim with care
At parking spaces I select
And hope the cars already there
Won't get a flaky side effect.

SITE UNSEEN

If someone named, when we were kids,
This town or that, we proudly stated,
"We drove through there!" This fed our ids
And made us feel sophisticated.
Such ego-boosters now are few.
When someone mentions Centerline,
Atlanta, Portland, Troy, Peru,
Kids say, "I saw the Exit sign."

INSIDE STORY

Beside your stomach may be seen
A pulpy organ called the spleen.
The body seems to perk without it
But, since its role is still in doubt, it
Is prudent on the part of man
To keep it in him if he can.
There once existed foolish notions
About the spleen and man's emotions
But these have now gone out of fashion.
You cannot blame the spleen for passion.

R. S. V. P.

A lot of people seem obsessed
With getting loads and loads of rest.
The doubt occurs, regarding some,
What they are resting for or from.

YOU AND YOURS – THE WRAP-UP

The human owns a bag, called skin,
To carry his components in.
It's fairly smooth, with here and there
Outcroppings such as nails and hair.
Of varied lengths and color tones,
It houses muscles, organs, bones,
Blood cells, and all that other stuff
That keeps man going well enough.
Without this comprehensive casing
He might forever be misplacing
Some vital part, or losing juices
From unprotected streams and sluices.
Though skin would make quite puny leather,
It helps man keep things all together.